# Energetic healing for beginners

*Easily understand energetic healing, apply it your-self or find a suitable healer*

*-incl. the examples of Reiki, Spiritual Healing, Homeopathy, Schuessler's Salts, Bach Flower Remedies, Psychokinesiology, Akashic Chronicle and EFT*

## Paula Friedberg

# Content

# What you can expect in this book

**This little guide is written for those interested in approaching the topic of "Energetic Healing" for the first time. Join me on a journey into the world of the holistic, energetic way of seeing and healing, the ideas of the energetic healers about the structure of our universe and the human being as an energetic being.**

In this small book I would like to give you a first insight into the world of energetic healing. We dive into the world of energy and information, into the human image of energetic healers, look at scientific attempts to explain the how and what of our world and the thinking of healers.

Visualize with me some different ways to stimulate, support and direct our self-healing powers.

If the scientific explanation models seem too theoretical for you, you are not interested in them or you have an aversion to physics and models, then please just keep on scrolling. I will try to bring you closer to the subject even without these models and maybe, if you should discover energetic healing as a possible way for yourself, one day the need will develop in you to learn more about the possible "behind". One just does, another wants to understand in order to be able to fully surrender to things. Whatever type you are, what counts is to go HIS way. There is no right and no wrong, only done or only thought.

Of course, it is not possible and would not do justice to the seriousness of the subject of health to present here the claim of a complete compendium of energetic healing. The ways, approaches, views of people are so different and broad that please do not expect a comprehensive "textbook". You will certainly not find listed one or another method that you have heard about or that you have already tried. Especially when we move away from the narrow path of scientifically proven methods and think outside the box, we will not be able to capture everything and cover it in this book. I therefore concentrate on an introduction to the subject and some methods, which you may use one day for yourself as a client or for self-application and in the family circle.

Once you have opened yourself to the subject and once you have started with one or the other, you will quickly continue to search and find. You will meet other people who will bring you on new paths and / or accompany you, use the Internet with its almost unlimited supply of information, read books about the different healing methods and spiritual paths. Every path begins with the first step.

At this point I would like to share with you a guiding principle that has accompanied me ever since I read it with a healer friend of mine and that has always brought me back to my path when I once struggled with my actions and their results:

---

**"There is a time for everything."**

---

# What is energetic Healing?

We will not find a scientific definition, because we will also search in vain for a "scientific explanation" or a "scientific proof" for healing with energy and information, at least according to the generally still prevailing models and views. So let's approach the definition from the healers' point of view.

# Definitions from the perspective of an energetic healer

Energetic healing is not a standardized or protected term. Basically, every healer, as well as every self-user, can call his "laying on of hands", his special gift of listening, comfort-giving, spiritual working, Reiki-giving etc. energetic and see it that way for himself, if he wants to.

Some practitioners also speak of "information medicine" in connection with energetic healing methods. Thus, we sometimes encounter this terminology among doctors who have expanded or specialized their field of activity and, for example, kinesiologically test homeopathic, spagiric or other remedies (more on this later), find out suitable beliefs or work with "informed water", to name just a few examples. But also alternative practitioners use this term. With self-users and spiritual healers you will hardly find this term, because only doctors and alternative practitioners are allowed to practice "healing" and so a demarcation is very important also in the wording for users who do not belong to these two professions. They are not allowed to "make healing promises", not to make diagnoses and not to practice "Heilkunde". What is to be understood by this is defined by the law.

Here, the "Law on the professional practice of medicine without a medical certificate" (Heilpraktiker-gesetz, abbreviated to HPG) from 1939 still applies. *(Heilpraktikergesetz, abbreviation HPG).*

Section 1 of the HPG states that:
*(Sourcewww.gesetze-im-internet.de/heilprg/__1.html)*

*"(1) Anyone wishing to practice medicine without being a licensed physician shall require permission to do so.*

*(2) The practice of medicine within the meaning of this Act shall mean any professional or commercial activity to diagnose, cure, or alleviate disease, suffering, or physical injury in humans, even if performed in the service of others."*

I would like to give you the view of an energetic healer and life coach, as he describes it to his clients: (*Source_www.zwei-strich-sinus.de/heilen.html*)

*"You can understand energetic healing as a summary description for healing procedures, where e.g. information or energy is transferred with the hands, often without any physical contact. Also the work with symbols, color glasses, on meridians, chakras and much more takes place on the "energetic", "informative" level."*

In an information folder for patients, the healer describes his work like this:

*(Source_Maik Gollas, life coach and energetic healer, info folder for patients 2014)*

*"As a rule, we understand by it (spiritual healing is meant, d. V.) the most diverse kinds of healing, in which, for example:*
- *it is assumed that "everything that is" consists of energy.*
- *the human being is not reduced to a biochemical-physical being, but is seen and also treated as a unity of body, mind and soul.*

## What does the energetic healer see me as?

Most energetic healers see you as a holistic being, consisting of matter surrounded by its own energy bodies, in the sense of multiple layers, and perceive you "holistically". Holism is the doctrine of the whole, where "holos", coming from the Greek, means "whole". The crucial meaning here is that holistically, "the whole is more than the sum of its parts."

Let me give you a small example of different ways of looking at the same thing.

Imagine you are standing in a gallery and you are looking at the exhibits. You are looking at a beautiful painting, which shows a picturesque landscape. On a small bench standing at the side of the road sits, slumped and seemingly powerless, an elderly gentleman with hat, which clutches his walking stick, which he can apparently hardly still hold

His gaze is fixed expressionlessly on the ground, his hands marked by seemingly decades of hard work, his head bowed by the many burdens of life, his eyes dull because they have seen so long and so much. Loneliness and sadness speak to you from every color pigment with which the painter has immortalized the old man.

Right out of the clouds comes a white ray of light, which hits this old gentleman and you think to yourself, ...

I leave it up to you how you interpret this picture, your heart will show you the way.

Suddenly, next to you, an employee of the gallery, neatly dressed in a bright white coat, begins to talk and snaps you out of your thoughts. You can't help overhearing his voice, he is standing right next to you, talking about the same painting that you, lost in thought, have been touching all this time with your eyes, your heart, maybe even (without anyone seeing) gently with your hands. The employee explains to another visitor:

*"We have before us a piece of canvas, 60 by 80 cm square in size. The canvas is framed by a frame made of wood of grade 1, cut in Canada in October 2018. The*

The whole thing increases in the further to describe the picture also fully.

When you hear this interpretation of the painting, do you feel it does justice to the overall work of art? Is the painting well described, expressing what it really is?

Sure, this picture wouldn't be this picture if more red and less green had been used. But is that all? Could you guess from the interpretation of the gallery employee what the painting expresses? What mood it affects, what it radiates, and what is really the most decisive thing about the painting as a whole? Certainly not the place of origin of the frame wood.

You perceive more in the painting than the employee. However, you could not prove your perception scientifically. Or?

And the human being can be viewed and treated just as differently. The holistically thinking physician and alternative practitioner will not only pay attention to the laboratory and the symptoms, he will look at the entire being with its emotions, its traumas, energetic, environmental, nutritional, etc. components. components. components.

The energetic healer, who does not belong to these professions, will perceive you in his own way and strengthen your self-healing powers. Whether through the laying on of hands or remote healing, through a spiritual approach in which your soul, your soul plan, comes up, or by painting signs on you. He may analyze your dealing with recurring problems in life and perhaps he will explain to you that you are the creator of your world outside.

Depending on your point of view, your path will in turn lead you to a healer of this or that kind. If the time is not yet ripe, you may go home dissatisfied. Maybe only at first, to realize later, "he wasn't so wrong about that". Or you will be on the same wavelength with your healer right away, accept and develop when the time is ripe.

The energetic healer usually follows more or less consciously or unconsciously, depending on his world view, the view that ultimately everything consists of energy and information. This energy he tries to bring back to flow and in harmony, to restore the "order". For this purpose he uses, among other things, the transmission of information. Whether by "informed water", Körblerische signs, laying on of hands, discussing or other, depends on his method.

So the energetic healer sees you in the first place not as a purely material, biochemical being whose symptoms have to be eliminated, but as a complex, energetic being, which he wants to support and heal more or less also on this level.

Depending on the career, development and imprinting, the energetic healer will follow this view to some extent or fully. So you can meet healers who are still very much attached to the structural, i.e. the material part of the body and the point of view, but can definitely do a lot for you, but also healers who are very spiritually imprinted and will talk to you more about your spiritual development, your soul and you as the creator of your reality.

## Does energetic healing work or is it all hocus-pocus?

For an energetic healer and the vast majority of his patients or clients this question does not arise. The healer knows about his successes, the patient or client experiences what changes or not after a visit with him. After that he will make his decision. But there is one thing we should be aware of when making our own decision: a tooth that has been knocked out will not grow back, an intestine that has been maltreated for decades will not heal in one session. And then there is the small but important instance: "What do I need my illness for?"

One thing you should not expect when you walk a path on the way of energetic healing is that you will hand over a body with problems and take back a body and a life without problems. You may be happy when your pain is quickly gone, the cause of long suffering has been found, the realization for recurring events is there, but there is usually a longer way ahead to become truly healed. Healing in the sense of "being whole and at one with yourself." Your body will probably send you a lifetime of symptoms as a signal and language from the subconscious. But working with it takes you beyond the purpose of this book.

I would like to give you a little insight into a point of view, which may help you to analyze your symptoms. Not everyone can and will follow this view, but that is not my intention.

Imagine that your body is the shell for your soul or, if you don't like it, just there for you, the part that you really are. Since you can observe yourself, your body, your actions, you cannot be your body at the same time.

So let's assume something, which you may name as you wish, inhabits this, your body. Maybe that's enough for now. ¶ This body speaks to you. About aches, then pains, later bigger limitations. But also through things that happen to you in life again and again, your body tries to make you aware of something you should change in your life. You will have the same experiences again and again, but always "louder". Some things run through your life like a thread and you keep asking yourself, "Why me, why me of all people?" If you overhear or ignore his signs, he will send you a bigger problem. Be that as it may, if we follow this thesis, you have with the symptom a mouthpiece of your soul. You only have to learn to understand it.

More on this perhaps in another book, it takes us too far away from the title of this book. But perhaps you will understand why it is sometimes not possible to cure certain symptoms or only to postpone them. If the causes are not removed, the symptoms will come back, one way or another. To become healed means first and foremost to recognize and work on yourself. Those who study more about this subject and this point of view can see that we always draw into our lives what we need in order to be able to develop. We are the transmitter, the others resonate with us or not. Or another "sends" and we go with him in resonance or not.

One good thing about all this is that we alone can change what we send out and we alone can determine whether this or that continues to cross our path. So we can draw beautiful things into our lives, but also continue the "red thread" that has been following us for a long time.

It is not up to the others, it is up to us. If we switch off our ego, our judgmental mind and recognize this, we become creators of another outside, which meets us.

At this point we end our little excursion into the world of symptom interpretation, the "language of the body" and man as creator. If you are interested in this, I refer you to the books of Ruediger Dahlke and, going one step further, Kurt Tepperwein. There are countless books and impressive videos by both of them, which can certainly give the one or the other reader a new perspective.

There is a large number of people who, after they were "out-treated" by conventional medicine, found the partner in an energetically working healer or alternative practitioner who relieved them of their suffering or at least made it more bearable. You can read many case studies on the Internet (more about this source later) or books by people who have written down their story of suffering accordingly. We can't project these to all cases, we can't claim it de facto, but a way that can be walked is all the same. And I am sure through my own journey and research on this book that one day we will be able to explain exactly why. For my part, I found the explanation a long time ago, but it is a process and a development that everyone should experience for themselves.

However, if today, perhaps in order to be able to make a decision for yourself, you need a scientifically based explanation and "proof" of energetic healing, with scientific evidence in the sense of

*"1000 people had this problem, 500 people of the experimental group were treated with the same Körbleric sign painted or that hand posture or that homeopathic remedy - over 450 of the participants treated in the same way showed an improvement of their symptoms up to*

you will be disappointed. We or a part of us are not that far yet. And in my opinion it would also contradict the view and approach of alternative healers and the basics of the work of energetic healing. Because just a remedy (homeopathy) tuned to the concrete being human in its totality, not limited to the symptom, the right vibration in resonance, that exactly to this person with this cause of one and the same symptom with several, excludes an equal treatment of many people with identical treatment method. One and the same energetic remedy cannot have the same effect on all people with the same symptoms. A person is more than his symptom.

The question also arises, why did the "barrel" overflow? Our body absorbs many things over time. Birth trauma, emotional wounding, stress in everyday life, environmental toxins, malnutrition, alcohol, ciga-rette, antibiotics, just to name a few. In addition, a great many people suffer from acute or chronic diseases and changes in the digestive tract. They can no longer tolerate many foods, react allergically. Crohn's disease, ulcerative colitis, histamine intolerance (HIT), sorbitol intolerance (SI), gluten sensitivity, the list has become longer and longer in recent years.

Deficiencies of basic vitamins, minerals, trace elements and more develop. The detoxification organs are overloaded or "grow with their tasks", see our liver.

And then, one day, when the barrel is full to the brim, one drop is enough to make it overflow. Whoever now looks only for the last drop, for example the virus, and restricts himself in the treatment only to this, will not heal the human being.

He will suppress the symptom, just like someone who removes only the top, small drop from the barrel. You can imagine for yourself what will happen the next time it rains a little. Transferring this, I mean that if your system was before tipping over and a small trigger (a virus or even bad news) caused it to overflow, i.e. fall, it will not get better if you only take care of the last "trigger". Not if you really want to "get well".

From a holistic point of view, and this is followed by most energetic healers who work "with input", i.e. not just as a pure channel for energy, you should first find out what makes up the largest amount, the largest chunk in your "barrel". What takes up the most space? What weakens your "human system" the most? What has filled your barrel (let's stick with this figurative example) so full that not even the drop could fit in? Does it make sense to remove the drop from the barrel when it is full to the brim with all kinds of garbage?

Precisely for this reason, because a holistically thinking healer, an energetic healer, will not only take care of the last drop, but of the barrel itself, he cannot take only one remedy for the drop of 10, 100, 1000 people who have been overflowed by the drop (virus), but will search until he has located the largest chunks in the barrel and then choose the appropriate tool with which he can remove these chunks.

Bring this once into a scientific study, as described above. How is this supposed to work with the understanding of a "scientific proof" which is still prevailing in the broad public today? What is needed in these things is a different basis of understanding, a different view of things than it is currently still conveyed to us as standard and which many people still follow alone in forming their opinions.

I have experienced it again and again that people have looked for all kinds of explanations, only not to have to admit what they experienced in their own bodies, namely that the energetic work worked. They were able to walk again, the injured thumb (several weeks old sports injury) was free of symptoms overnight, a kinesiological arm length test indicated what only they could know etc. Especially from very "top-heavy" people, mostly from the studied area, it is often not possible to assume what just happened.

It does not fit into the world view. Many people also don't like to talk about the fact that they have been to an energetic healer, a spiritual healer, a psychokinesiologist. The shame of what others might think of you plays a role. There the simplest things were talked to pieces and tried to explain with probabilities, placebo, expectation etc.. If only some people knew what sense of achievement they were depriving themselves of.

## Scientific Models or "How Does Energetic Healing Work?"

There are explanatory approaches, studies, written treatises, lectures at congresses and much more, in which attempts are made to explain the work, the ascertainable effects of the actions of energetic healers or energetic healing methods with current scientific models. In recent years, the following approach has crystallized.

---

## Everything vibrates - everything is energy

---

Our world consists of (data slightly different):

5 % visible matter

25 % dark matter

70% invisible energy.


So let's first take note of the fact that, according to scientific consensus, only 5% of our world consists of what we perceive with our "normal" senses and interpret as "what is".

Let's keep in mind further that an atom, which we are all familiar with and which we hold "responsible" as the basic building block for our matter, consists of 99.9999999% "empty space".

*(Source_Dr. Ulrich Warnke, Quantum Philosopher,*

*https://magazin-fo-*

*rum.de/de/news/leben/%C2%84wir-bestehen-zu-99-pro-*

*zent-aus-vakuum%C2%93)*

You haven't read it wrong, there's the number 99 with another nine nines after the decimal point. So we consist of 99.9999999 % vacuum. Hard to imagine, isn't it? Other publications regularly mention only 99.9999 %, but I don't think that this is significant for our point of view. But it is quite amazing, if matter consists of more than 99 % of nothing, this means that we also consist of more than 99 % of nothing. So we perceive with our "normal" senses only 5% of the present, which consists of over 99% of nothing. A scary idea.

As an illustrative example, a soccer field is often taken as a size comparison for the ratio of the atomic nucleus to the atomic shell (orbiting electrons). The atomic nucleus corresponds to a pinhead in the middle of a soccer field and the shell represents the outer line of the field.

This makes it rather clear what these 99.9999999% mean.

But it goes on. Still in my school time the atom was considered according to the curriculum as "last indivisible particle", to be traced back to the atom model of Democritus. Then came the discoveries that the atomic nucleus consists of protons and neutrons, subatomic particles, quarks, quantum physics became known and better known, string theory appeared on the scientific horizon and much more.

Protons and neutrons, for example, consist of the named quarks. As a source of information for further study I can recommend here, among other things, "Ecosystem Earth - The Structure of Matter" *(https://www.oekosystem-erde.de/html/exkurs-02.html).*

The further science goes into the smallest particles, the more it enters the realm of fields, waves and oscillations, which then reads like this, for example:

*"Because of their quantum nature, subatomic particles cannot be thought of as classical particles. Rather, quantum phenomena such as wave-particle duality, uncertainty relations, vacuum fluctuations, and virtual particles appear in the physical description of the behavior and reactions of subatomic particles.¶*

The practitioners of information medicine and energetic healing draw for themselves from the various scientific findings and models of thought the essence that ultimately everything is made up of vibrations. Dr. Masaru Emoto, a Japanese researcher, observed frozen water crystals and found that water changed when exposed to words, thoughts, music. Positive words or thoughts, melodic music, resulted in beautiful, symmetrical water crystals. If the water was exposed to negative thoughts, insults or heavy metal music, the water crystals were chaotic to the point of breaking.

Humans are made up of about 70% water. How do you think different, information, vibrations, also mobile phone waves affect this part of the body?

There are users who "inform" water and then take sips. Those who talk to their plants and are happy to see them thrive will be able to follow me.

There are many questions, many models and many explanations, but in the end there are still no doubtless answers which would last forever.

Interesting are approaches from quantum physics. For example, a contribution from the Max Planck Society entitled "Quantum particles in synchronous dance" describes

*"As if by magic, seemingly independent pendulum clocks can come together to tick simultaneously and synchronously. The phenomenon of 'self-organized synchronization' often occurs in nature and technology and is a core research area of Marc Timme's team at the Max Planck Institute ..."*

*"The examples are not limited to mechanical oscillations. "This also occurs in many different biological networks," Timme explains, "In the brain, the phenomenon occurs in the synchronization of nerve impulses."'*

Only yesterday I saw a vivid video with an experimental setup in which a person had hung two tennis balls over a tuning fork with 440 Hz, which were attached to the side of this. If he struck a second tuning fork near this one, which was calibrated to a different frequency, nothing happened. As soon as he struck a tuning fork that also vibrated at 440 Hz, the permanently mounted tuning fork went into resonance, which could be seen from the bouncing tennis balls.

Who would like to deal a little more with the matter, should deal with the current cosmological models, quantum physics or quantum mechanics, string theory and other models. There you will find some interesting approaches, which are quite interesting as an explanation for an effect of energetic healing and information medicine. Also I stand on the point of view, finally everything is energy and information. And so a practiced healer can feel into another person, perceive what the environment does not see and a medical apparatus cannot yet detect. In the information field things can show up which are not yet manifested on the physical level.

How often are we "on the same wavelength" with someone or not, can "smell" them or not? Do you know that when someone says something that triggers us, that appeals to us? Or, on the contrary, we don't give a damn?

In the first case we go into resonance, something speaks to us. The other person has hit the sore spot. In the second case, nothing of the sort happens. A piece of information comes and hits nothing that resonates. We do not respond to it.

## Self-healing powers

We experience it again and again that our body heals itself. It fights pathogens, deals with viruses, bacteria, fungi and others. It allows wounds to heal, detoxifies our body and eliminates. You don't have to define it, our body has the ability to heal itself and is basically programmed to heal itself.

However, there are also situations in which our body with its own power to heal itself does not get anywhere. Also, the self-healing powers can be severely weakened to almost completely come to a standstill. Then the slightest cause, otherwise no problem for our body, is enough to overturn the system. Therapists also know the phenomenon of the healing blockade.

You may have already observed this in yourself. You go to the doctor, alternative practitioner, osteopath or energetic healer and, no matter what efforts they make, your body just won't respond. Treatment, whether conventional (if not aimed exclusively at eliminating symptoms) or by a therapist, does not work. The otherwise existing reactions to treatment do not take place. Many a therapist then resigns, as does the patient or client himself. Here it is necessary to uncover the causes of the healing blockages.

Are there still larger blockages, emotional, toxic, traumas or other stresses that need to be worked through beforehand so that the body can react again at all? Can it come back into its self-regulation? Here, for example, kinesiological testing has proven very useful in practice.

Or does the patient/client from the viewpoint of "illness as a path" still need these symptoms? "Illness as a path" describes the view that our body is the mouthpiece of our subconscious, our soul. It communicates to us through symptoms what we do not see, feel, hear, understand.

**An example to illustrate**

Over the course of time, a patient develops ever greater movement restrictions until she is finally no longer able to walk. The general practitioner refers her to an orthopedist, who, after a thorough examination and without a diagnosis, refers her to a neurologist. The neurologist, also unable to find a diagnosis, advises the patient to see a psychologist, saying that the problem is "psychosomatic" and that there is no physical, structural or biochemical explanation.

The patient reaches, possibly after another long way, a therapist who questions things differently. He listens to the life story and circumstances of his client, perhaps he also tests (psycho-) kinesiologically and thus gets answers directly from the subconscious of his client. In the end, it becomes clear and causal that the client feels very unwell at work, but has been pursuing this for years due to financial fears and has suppressed the signals of her body. Perhaps one also gets to the original trauma that the client was taught by her parents that she will only be financially secure and without risk firmly in life.

The patient knows, she feels that this work robs her of her strength, makes her joy of life dwindle, but "it has to be done" is firmly anchored in her thinking. And now her body begins to speak. It becomes the mouthpiece of her soul. In the beginning, it sent her listlessness, loss of appetite, a poor night's sleep. It was too little, the suffering pressure not great enough to bring about a change in her life. Then he sent knee pain, with which she continued to drag herself to work every day. When other symptoms, although treated, remained "unheard" or "misunderstood", he sent her immobility. Whether in the form of a herniated disc, pinched sciatica, or whatever, it was loud enough that it could no longer be ignored. The suffering pressure became so great that the client began to think completely about the meaning of her life for once.

Whether there is something else besides this work? Whether this is what life has in store for her? Whether there might not be another way and whether now is the time to really think about herself for once? And this does not mean the rent, food and other obligations, these must undoubtedly be served. But if the body is already screaming NO, is that still my way? Where have I gone, where have I lost myself along the way? Who am I? What am I? And above all, what do I still want to be, to experience, to achieve?

When the meanings of her symptoms are (made) clear to her, first her attitude, her self-perception changes. She comes more and more into consciousness and asks life other questions. And she draws a line. She goes to work and clearly states to the boss where her boundaries are from now on and draws them for her boss and many a colleague as well. And she reveals to him that she will look for another job. A job that fulfills her, in which she is valued and which also makes her smile during the day.

I am telling this story because I was able to share in it. Whether her entire work environment changed or she found fulfillment in a new job, I don't know. But she was able to walk again, and pain-free. She smiled again and built self-confidence. The cause, better, what the body was trying to tell her, had gone away.

There had been a change in the mind and thus this symptom was no longer necessary.

What do these and countless other similar experiences from practice tell us? We can block or heal ourselves and have a decisive influence on it. Our thinking, our actions, our ideas, views, beliefs, conception of who we are, have an effect on our body. And so it is not surprising when patients, after sometimes long periods of therapy without success, suddenly experience healing through a conversation, a look into the subconscious, a spiritual counseling, etc. experience healing.

Even a scar on a meridian can have a tremendous impact. Movement restrictions, lack of energy, heart problems, gastrointestinal problems. If these scars are

recognized and cleared, sometimes the most unbeliev-
able things happen.

There are many things that can interfere with the self-healing of our body. And many methods to find and work on them.

The goal of the energetic healer will always be to support this self-healing.

# Some examples of known methods of energetic healing

Among the best known energetic healing methods are Reiki, spiritual healing, various applications of kinesiology, work on the aura and chakras, as well as talking, work with stones, Schuessler salts, homeopathy, but also many lesser known approaches and methods. Depending on how far you move from the materialistic to the spiritual, you can continue this list. Psychokinesiology, systemic family constellation according to Bert Hellinger, reading

**in the Akashic Chronicle, quantum healing - the world of energetic healing is large.**

## Reiki

Reiki is a Japanese artificial word and means universal life energy. It consists of the characters "rei", for mind or soul, spiritual, but also "the whole" and "ki", for life energy (also known as "chi").

According to legend, the "rediscovery" of Reiki goes back to the Japanese scholar **Mikao Usui** (1865 to 1926), who spent his life searching for a method to strengthen his body and mind. He knew from ancient writings that this was possible energetically, but that it required an initiation, but he did not know how to obtain it. In 1922, Usui, as a Buddhist, is said to have had an enlightenment experience during a 21-day meditation on the holy mountain of Kurama, as a result of which he developed "**Usui-Reiki**".

Usui-Reiki represents for many Reiki practitioners the entry into the world of Reiki, but also of energetic healing itself. Usui-Reiki is primarily passed on through direct initiation into degrees by a Reiki Master/Teacher and works with symbols. Usui-Reiki is generally described by both users and receivers as a very gentle energy.

In the course of the last years a limited number of degrees (3rd degree = Master) became more and more, today we find initiation offers up to the 21st degree. They are supposed to be an extension of the Usui system and to be light or grand master degrees.

What to think of it, everyone must decide for themselves, what remains is the pure energy, which, given by the right healer, will do the right thing. As always in life, it depends on meeting the right person at the right moment. Never let degrees and colorful certificates guide your decision. We will still go into the topic of "How to find my healer".

Another very well known form of Reiki is "**Kundalini Reiki**". Kundalini Reiki goes back to the ascended **master Kuthumi** and was channeled through Ole Gabrielsen, a Danish meditation teacher. Kundalini-Reiki is mainly passed on through remote initiation, comes entirely without symbols and is perceived as a very powerful healing energy. Here too, through regular channeling by Ole Gabrielsen, a further development has taken place in recent years, through which the quality and strength of the

Kundalini energy has been adapted to the higher energy and vibration of the earth.

This resulted in the **Kundalini-Reiki-Millennium**, which includes further Reiki energies (Reiki-Balance, Diamond-Reiki, Crystalline-Reiki, DNA-Reiki, Birth Trauma-Reiki, Location-Reiki and Past-Life-Reiki). Kundalini-Reiki-Millennium is now passed on in a single initiation and includes the previous degrees 1 to 3 (incl. Master/Teacher) and the boosters I to III, making Kundalini-Reiki-Millennium currently the strongest Reiki system known to me.

However, I would not go to any Reiki giver who has been initiated exclusively into Millennium without first having completed a development in Kundalini Reiki accompanied by a teacher. Passing on Reiki means, as with every healer and therapist, to first work on oneself, to treat oneself and to come to terms with oneself. This is a journey and does not happen in 30 minutes. So look for the career and gladly also the family tree.

In addition, there are other Reiki systems such as Shamballa Reiki, Karuna Ki Reiki, Angel Ki Reiki, Gold Reiki and Full Spectrum Reiki, to name a few. Don't be fooled. The name of the system is less important, the focus should be solely on the person you are entrusting yourself to. And before you learn Reiki yourself, you will purposefully explore the systems and find the one(s) that are right for you.

For your own start, I would recommend one of the first two systems mentioned.

Common to both, as in Reiki in general, is that the Reiki giver does not give his own energy (unless he does it wrong, then he will regularly be weak himself after the treatment), but only acts as a channel for the corresponding energy. The Usui Reiki giver connects to the Reiki energy via the crown chakra for this purpose, the Kundalini Reiki giver connects to Mother Earth via the root chakra.

In order to be able to give Reiki, an initiation or "attunement" takes place in the various systems, in which the chakras and energy pathways are cleansed and opened. This is generally seen as a prerequisite to receive the corresponding energy as a channel and pass it on through his hand chakras. I would always advocate, whether direct or remote initiation, to look for a teacher/master in the corresponding Reiki system and to work together with him. There are also people who have retained their inherent ability to simply pass on energy. They feel the energy flow independently of an initiation and are often amazed at the beginning what they achieve with others without having "learned" it.

For example, children are often still able to perceive the aura (the energy field) around people. Ask a child when they draw bright colors around the head and body of painted people why they do this. I have often witnessed children talking about these clouds of color they saw around people. Children see beings that we do not perceive (anymore).

The saddest case I know of was when a little girl held a bird imaginary for the adults on her hands and proudly showed it to them. The father, who had no access, clapped both hands and ... it marked the girl.

Never laugh at your children when you see or perceive something that is closed to you in your boundaries.

## Spirit healing

Spirit healing or the spiritual healer is for most people the epitome of the energetic healer. When you observe a spiritual healer at work, you will smile ignorantly at first. With a Reiki practitioner, many can still apply that he is channeling and transmitting life energy. The hand positions are partly still comprehensible for an "ignorant" person. ¶The first contact with a spiritual healer is usually somewhat different. At (mostly spiritual) fairs, exhibitions or other events they stand or sit next to likewise standing, sitting or even lying participants. They "see" and "hear" things which we at first think are impossible because we do not perceive them ourselves. They discuss warts, work with one-handed rods or rods that have electrodes on one side. With these they scan the bodies of the participants. Still other spiritual healers work in pairs on their clients.

Two of the most famous spiritual healers in Germany are **Horst Krohne** and the already deceased **Bruno Gröning** (1906 to 1959). Bruno Gröning treated countless people, gave many lectures and explained his work by a healing current sent by God and passed on to people through him. Throughout his life and beyond, Bruno Gröning faced the most severe hostility and state sanctions. His followers and countless "healed" people loved him and still revere him today. Thus, even today, he is sometimes described in articles as "The greatest spiritual healer of all time." Whether he was a miracle healer or a charlatan, I do not lose any thoughts about it. He brought relief and healing to many people in his time.

Horst Krohne, who is still active today and who trains healers himself, was a guest and answered questions in many rounds of talks on this subject and is the founder of the "School of Spiritual Healing®". He is still considered one of the most prominent spiritual healers in Europe.

Horst Krohne wrote countless books about spiritual healing:
- The House Book of Spirit Healing
- The School of Spirit Healing
- Healing hands
- Organ Speech Therapy
- Spirit healing - dialogue with the soul.

Just from this small selection of his books you can see in which direction the spiritual healing goes. He himself describes it in one of his books like this: (old spelling)

*"Healing, however, is not something that can be done - neither by spirit healing nor by medication or any conventional medical treatment methods. All that is*

*transmitted is information that leads to self-regulation. In this, the healer has the function of the teacher, who points out the cause of the suffering and stimulates healing."*

The field of spiritual healers is large and there are also some real charlatans in it. It is not easy to distinguish the good from the less good and the frauds.

Follow your heart, your gut, the experiences of others you can trust. Don't bring an unsum to someone you don't have a good feeling about, but try if your inner voice advises you to.

## Homeopathy

First of all, whether one assigns homeopathy to "energetic healing" depends on the viewpoint of the observer. I address it because it works with information in the subtle realm and thus corresponds to the basic mode of action of energetic healing. It is also attributed to the "regulation therapies", which are supposed to balance body and mind and activate the self-healing powers.

Homeopathy, composed of the Greek "homoios" and "pathos", meaning "similar" and "suffering", goes back to the German physician and pharmacist Samuel Hahnemann (1755 to 1843).

Hahnemann, dissatisfied with the prevailing methods of his professional colleagues at his time - bloodletting, emetic and laxative cures, the administration of medicines made of arsenic, lead or mercury were still common - discovered in self-experimentation and on other healthy test subjects (simplified) that medicines and natural substances cure in a sick person what they similarly cause in a healthy one. This "similarity rule" - *Similia similibus curentur or* "Simile principle", embodies the essence of homeopathy and was described by Hahnemann as "Let similar things be cured by similar things".

For each remedy in homeopathy there is a drug picture, which describes the effect in the healthy and sick. The available remedies, which consist of plants, minerals and animals, were and are found through the still valid "drug test", in which the vacant substance is given to the healthy person and then the resulting symptoms are recorded and result in the drug picture.

You can view drug images on the Internet at *https://www.homoeopathie-online.info/arzneimittel-bilder-in-der-homoeopathie/.*

Homeopathic remedies are found as globules and as drops (contain alcohol). They are "potentized", that is, they are in diluted form. You will find D potencies (1:10 each), C potencies (1:100) to extreme high potencies of CM (1:100$^{100.000}$ ). However, it is in homeopathy that the effectiveness does not decrease with the potentization = dilution, but the opposite occurs. The higher a remedy is potentized, the more it acts on the mental level and the more precisely the drug picture must fit the symptom. While the layman usually uses homeopathy in the potencies D6/D12, C30 and the D6/D12 potency acts rather broadly and more structurally, higher potencies require a precise selection and are sometimes used only in a single dose or with long pauses between the doses.

There are enough books and lists on the Internet for the home user. If you want to work purposefully, away from Arnica, Ruta, Apis and other remedies for the homeopathic emergency pharmacy, the way does not lead past a trained homeopath. He will have a long conversation with you to find the appropriate homeopathic remedy(s) and potencies for you.

The homeopath can also work on physical as well as mental symptoms and behavior patterns.

Briefly something about the effectiveness, which is often denied to homeopathy or attributed to the placebo effect: Just ask yourself why an effect in children and animals should be a placebo effect. If you are now open, try it. If, on the other hand, you start to formulate an explanation that yes animals and children are helped by their attachment to mother or owner ... etc., then don't, it's not your way. It could still help you, but do not do it to the homeopath.

## Schuessler salts

Here I will be a little briefer, if you have read the chapter on homeopathy you will see the similarities.

**Schüßler salts** are used as globules/tablets based on lactose and are usually available in the potencies D6 and D12. Dr. Schüßler himself, a homeopathic physician, discovered in his time (1821 to 1889) the Schüßler salts 1 to 12. In the course of time, 15 other supplementary salts were added to these basic salts and the range is still expanding.

While homeopathic remedies are mainly used in therapy for recovery, the Schuessler salts are often also used preventively. They are e.g. gladly taken with or for the avoidance of deficiency supplies, whereby they should not fall in these potencies as suppliers themselves into the weight, here they seem to function rather as door openers or initiators for the cells, whereby these are stimulated to take up the appropriate mineral materials themselves better from the food and to smuggle into the cells, so the way of thinking.

A classic and widely used application of Schuessler salts in home use, known even among laymen, is the "Hot 7". The Schüßler salt No. 7 is "Magnesium phosphoricum" and magnesium is known to have a relaxing effect on muscles and nature.

Thus, 10 globules/tablets of salt No. 7 are added to hot water, stirred with a non-metallic spoon and drunk in sips. This has a relaxing effect on cramps and the like. Just try it once and repeat it calmly at an interval at which you would also drink chamomile tea, for example, if you have gastrointestinal problems.

More information on the various Schuessler salts can be found, for example, at *www.schuessler-salze-portal.de/schuessler-salze-liste.html,* but many other sources are also helpful.

# Bach Flowers

Bach flower therapy goes back to the English physician and researcher Edward Bach (1886 to 1936), a pioneer of psychosomatic medicine, and has been systematically developed further by Mechthild Scheffer over the past 25 years.

Edward Bach discovered and developed a natural method, easy to use for everyone, to promote mental health and thus prevent physical illness.


*"The original Bach flowers are for the most part still collected today in the wild at the English sites specified by Edward Bach. 38 specially prepared flower extracts from wild growing plants and trees are used in individually composed "Bach flower mixtures". They are free of side effects and are compatible with every other form of conventional and naturopathic therapy.*

*Original Bach Flower Therapy is used today by many people for self-treatment and in numerous medically or psychologically oriented practices and institutions."*

*(Source_Workbook Bach Flowers, "Center for Holistic Development of Body, Mind and Soul")*

Bach flowers have three areas of application,

• mental health care

• Acute treatment of psychological stress situations and life crises

• Accompanying treatment of acute and chronic diseases.

Very well known in the "emergency pharmacy" is the remedy "Rescue Remedy", which, as the name suggests, is used primarily in emergencies and exceptional situations and consists of five Bach flowers. Whether exam anxiety, a visit to the dentist or a drastic, upsetting situation, if Bach flowers are part of your repertoire, this is the time for Rescue Remedy drops.

## New homeopathy according to Erich Körbler

With the new homeopathy according to Erich Körbler, one is initially tempted to think of a further development of homeopathy. But we are dealing here with a different approach. What both have in common is that they work on the information level.

The "New Homeopathy according to Erich Körbler" is also called "Medicine to paint on", because this method uses various symbols and signs, which are painted on the body, for example on scars.

Erich Körbler (1938 to 1994) was an electromechanic and developed this method from the "geometry medicine of the primitive peoples", as he himself called it. The power and effect of symbols and geometric signs has been known for millennia, they were already found in various primitive peoples and the mummy "Ötzi" discovered in 1991 in the Italian Similaun glacier, which is about 5000 years old.

By means of a tensor, for example the one-handed rod, the pendulum, but also by kinesiological testing, physical interference fields, incompatibilities, allergies and more are traced and then painted with the corresponding sign, which can also be tested. Thus, a reprogramming on the energetic level should take place.

Here I would like to describe an illustrative example from practice.

A woman has a large scar on her arm after a bicycle accident and, even after a long period of recovery, can barely move it up to chest level, which is where it ends. With this persistent restriction of movement, she seeks the help of an osteopath who, with a lot of experience and what I consider to be an excellent treatment method, gives the patient a range of movement up to head height in a relatively short time. But despite further treatment, the end is also reached here, it does not go further.

And now comes the exciting part: The osteopath asks the energetic healer present in the practice to take a look at the patient. With the patient's consent, the healer tests the large surgical scar and finds that it represents a disturbance on the meridian that crosses it. The energy in the meridian only reaches this scar and cannot flow further. The healer tests the strength of the disturbance with a one-handed rod and thereby determines the corresponding Körbleric sign, which he will paint on a short time later.

As a rule, the next step is to test how long an applied mark should remain. Here, in this specific case, the sign, even to the astonishment of the healer himself, already shows effect directly after application. The patient can immediately lift her arm above her head and this without pain.

This is certainly a special and quick result, but it shows how simple it can be sometimes.

By the way, the meridian system has been known for thousands of years, is an integral part of TCM (Traditional Chinese Medicine) and is indispensable to it. It is also used in acupuncture according to Penzel, acupressure and other related treatment methods.

The medicine for painting on or "new homeopathy according to Körbler" is ideal for the layman and self-user. There is countless literature on this, in which the individual signs and the procedure are well described.

## Psychokinesiology and systemic family constellations

Psychokinesiology (according to Dr. med. Dietrich Klinghardt) and systemic family constellation (according to Bert Hellinger) are methods which can go deep into the emotional world and with which you should only confide in a proven therapist.

In both systems, problems are "worked on" directly using inquiry techniques and guided by the therapist.

**Psychokinesiology (PK)** is a method often used when you confide in a therapist in an individual session and want to get to the bottom of the causes of physical and mental symptoms, recurring events, etc. and then work on them. The psychokinesiologist, with the help of the kinesiological muscle or arm length test, approaches your issue. Color glasses, eye movements and more are used to penetrate deeper layers, and also to find and resolve the "Unresolved Soul Conflicts" (USK), which are a fundamental thought process of PK. USKs, depending on their severity, dig themselves into the subconscious to varying degrees, and it takes some work to uncover them. This is partly because the subconscious mind protects itself from re-injury by re-experiencing the repressed emotions. Techniques from other psychoanalytic methods have also found their way into PK and are readily used. One example is the eye movement method mentioned above for resolving recognized USKs.

A **systemic family constellation (FA)** is mainly conducted in groups, only rarely as an individual session. In a group constellation, the participant (constellator) names his or her problem, such as smoking, constant fears, failure at work, illnesses, relationship problems, disturbed relationship with children and parents, and much more. The therapist appoints a representative from the group of participants, who takes the role of the constellator in the "constellation". Other participants become representatives for other people and things in the environment (usually the family of origin) of the constellator. They position themselves freely in the room and dive into this role within the morphogenetic field. They suddenly feel like the persons they represent. Now it is up to the therapist's abilities to work with them, to uncover and release energetic entanglements.

In both methods (PK and FA), the sessions very often get down to the "nitty-gritty". Old, repressed or never perceived traumas (also from previous lives) are relived and worked through. So in both cases you need an experienced therapist who can catch you and knows exactly what he is doing.

In addition to many good experiences with both methods, I would also like to tell you about a negative example. I personally experienced a family constellation in which the therapist (apparently influenced by her own experiences) massively suppressed the topic of abuse that arose in the constellation several times. This was confirmed to me by the constellating participant upon my perception and later inquiry. Another participant had perceived it in her case as well and told us about it.

Not only was the purpose of such a constellation of the family of origin completely lost sight of, but the unresolved problems of the participants remained and a great opportunity was lost. Also, this therapist did not properly "release" a representative from her role after the constellation. While the therapist sat at lunch, the proxy was shivering with fear and cold, huddled in a chair. She had taken on the role of the dead grandmother, in which she was still energetically with all these feelings and emotions.

What do I want to tell you with this? You can see from this negative example how far persons in the morphogenetic field can identify with the other, can reproduce him. A blessing in the hand of a good therapist and a curse at the same time, if you get to the wrong one.

Fortunately, this experience remained an isolated case and has not been repeated in other constellations with other therapists. So I would like to take away your fear again, that these experiences remained single cases. And in a systemic family constellation in a group you can also participate and gain experience only as a representative. This is a good way and recommended by me. Many participants then spontaneously decide to have their problems constellated themselves.

I can recommend both psychokinesiology and systemic family constellation if you find a good therapist, but would advise you to read up on this method beforehand, especially in the case of family constellation, or to talk to a former participant.       ¶ For example,

I have accepted two lost siblings, whom I was never allowed to meet, but who played a drastic role in my life and in one of these constellations, for me and was able to say goodbye to them.

## EFT - Emotional Freedom Technique

**EFT, in German the "techniques for emotional freedom", are an excellent tool for self-application.**

EFT is a therapeutic concept of "energetic psychology". Originally based on the findings and experiences of clinical psychologist Roger J. Callahan from the 1970s and 1980s and called Thought-Field-Therapy (TFT), his student, the American **Gary Craig**, developed Emotional Freedom Technique (EFT) from it in 1984.

Callahan himself first applied his form of therapy to the treatment of phobias and later expanded it to a variety of other disorders.

EFT is colloquially known as the "tapping technique" and this already describes the basic procedure. You will tap meridian points on your body with your fingers during EFT (self) treatment. A good therapist will explain this method to you and give you a tool for self-application. Helping yourself is the motto.

In addition to EFT, you may also come across the term "MET" in your search. For one thing, MET is the name for "Meridian Energy Therapies" in the English-speaking world and EFT is one method of it. "M.E.T. according to Franke®" on the other hand is copyrighted because Rainer Franke, originally from the EFT community, calls his tapping therapy that. If you want to know something about the "differences" and reasons or "constraints" for this "renaming", you will find it on the Internet. *(https://emofree.ch/haeufig-gestellte-fragen)*

You can find far more and freely accessible information on EFT on the Internet, it is neither protected, nor heavily commercialized.

By the way,

*"In the spring of 2012, EFT was recognized as an "evidence-based method" by the APA (American Psychological Association) as a science-based method of therapy."* *(www.eft-info.com)*

# Stones, "informed water" and other things

In the world of energetic healing, as already described, it is assumed that in the smallest part everything vibrates and everything is information. So also stones, colors and much more.

Colors can be found, for example, in the form of the color glasses in kinesiology.

**Stone healing** has a long tradition. There is an almost unmanageable amount of discovered healing stones, which are especially well described in the books of the alternative practitioner and psychotherapist Werner Kühni. I refer to his books:

- Encyclopedia of stone medicine
- Pocket encyclopedia of healing stones.

Werner Kühni runs the first healing stone museum with store in Stockheim, is trained in classical homeopathy and works as a non-medical practitioner specializing in stone healing.

As a rule, healing stones are used for self-treatment or by spiritually oriented therapists. If you are again once on a market on the way, on which also different stones are offered, take nevertheless once such a "Handschmeichler" in the hand and feel into it. Maybe you suddenly feel a warmth, a sense of well-being. Then it is "your" stone. Look then once on the usually lying small descriptions to this stone. It could be that you feel addressed.

**Water** is considered in medicine not only the most important, first and most necessary element for our body. You can go without food for a few days, you can build up a deficiency of this or that mineral, vitamin, trace element over a longer period of time, but you can survive only a short period of time without water. I do not want to go further into the function of water for our body from a biochemical point of view.

In the context described in this book it is about water as information storage and transmitter. As already described in chapter 2.4 using the example of Dr. Masaru Emoto, water, depending on external influences, takes on certain forms, vibration patterns, cluster structures, which remain for a time until other influences change them. And so therapists and self-users used water, for example, to supply it with desired information and thus bring it into the body. It is assumed that in this way, among other things, our cells can be informed.

One discusses his glass of water, the other puts it on a piece of paper on which the desired information is written. Other methods are holding the water in one hand and a substance (e.g. a homeopathic one) in the other. Then one visualizes the transition of the information from the initial object to the water. There are various methods and it is worthwhile for the interested person to study them further. It costs almost nothing, is quickly at hand and no harmful substances are absorbed, unless one takes bad, polluted water itself.

## Akashic Chronicle

I would not like to withhold from you one possibility, which I was also allowed to get to know and experience personally. The reading (let) in his Akasha Chronicle.

Please try to leave all "valuations" out of it for once. We are here, in this book, with some methods anyway in an area which may seem hardly imaginable for many, for others with their faith and their "scientific understanding" absurd. But it is not my aim to convince you of this way of thinking and perception. I understand this book as an offer for interested people to dive once into this world. Not everybody has to go every way.

Back to the Akashic Chronicle. According to the practitioners, this is an information field that surrounds and permeates all of us, the entire universe and perhaps beyond, in which all information about everything that has ever happened, all thoughts, emotions, events, is stored. It is a huge library of all being.

Also the information about what will happen for the individual, under the aspect of the "snapshot", is included. Since we are all creators of our being, we have at any time the free decision to do something this way or that way. So we can determine ourselves whether what will happen at the moment as a result of our "being like this" will then actually "stay like this", in the sense of "will happen", or whether we manifest it differently as creators. Already with a reading and the "becoming conscious", what is, something changes in us and therefore the future.

Be that as it may, with a reading (Reading) in your Akashic Chronicle you can gain insights into processes in your life that were previously inaccessible to you. It is a journey into the unconscious, into that which cannot be perceived with the mind.

What determines my life? What are my self-made walls socially and in the work environment? How do I deal with desires, emotions? What am I not "living"? What am I doing that contradicts my desire as a soul? Where are my hidden traumas and what are they?

You can meet your inner child, contacts with deceased, ascended masters or your spirit guides can arise. You can experience what your old relationships, spouses, friendships and enmities still have for energetic links with you. You can realize what your soul, your true "I" really wants. This will always remain hidden from your mind. And you can work on all of this.

The first contact with the library of life usually takes place through a reading by another person. Then often arises the desire to gain access to the Akashic Chronicle for oneself and others. In principle, it is possible for everyone to enter it and read in it. However, for many people it will remain hidden for the rest of their lives. However, those who embark on their spiritual journey will sooner or later hear about it and request access. Then the right book, the right person will enter his life.

I recommend as literature the book by Gabrielle Orr,

● "Akashic Chronicle One True Love, The Practical Guide to Reading the Book of Life."

I can only say it is a beautiful experience that I would not want to miss.

If you want to develop and become whole, at some point you have to face your inner child, your hurts, your buried traumas and feelings. But once you have climbed to the top, you will have an unobstructed view of the sun and your life will change fundamentally.

I wish you a good trip, if you want to.

# Who is energetic healing aimed at?

## What is the target audience for energetic healing?

There is no specific target group from the healer's point of view. Everyone who sets foot in the practice of an energetic healer or wants to take advantage of his offer for remote healing will be welcome first. Of course, it matters how you feel about energetic healing, whether you give the healer and yourself a chance. If you visit an energetic healer full of reservations and not openly, you are boycotting yourself in the first place. If he lays his hands on you and you refuse inside, your time has not come yet.

It may be that the energy flows anyway, but it is just as possible, and this is my experience, that the energy is not there for you then.

There are different possibilities here. The universal life energy Reiki will perhaps flow, the energies, which a spiritual healer "uses", perhaps rather not. There is no reason to heal a person who is not yet ready for it, because he still needs his symptoms and therefore "sabotages" himself. This denial, called "self-sabotage", takes place in the subconscious, often completely unnoticed by the client.

More about this in the next chapter.

## Energetic healing - my way?

The ways to become an energetic healer or energetic healing as a self-user are diverse, just as people are diverse. Whether someone as a patient goes the way to an energetic healer, energetic working doctor, healer or Reiki practitioner depends on several circumstances, much on his attitude and experience.

Experience shows that anyone who is on the spiritual path is more likely to see an alternative practitioner than a doctor. Those who have never or only little dealt with these topics, their first visit will almost always lead them to a doctor.

Then there are, for example, patients who are considered "out of treatment", for whom no causes can be "found", who are "psychosomatic" or receive a diagnosis at the limit of hope. Often there are long histories of suffering behind them and the people feel helpless because improvement can no longer be expected. Then, not infrequently, their apparent hopelessness leads them to other approaches and they try out possibilities that were previously rather ridiculed.

So if you are open to new ways and can also just allow once, even if no studied doctor sits opposite you, if you do not have to think through everything and understand it scientifically, then use the chance that may present itself. ¶If, on the other hand, you try and are still full of rejection, you will first and foremost do yourself no favors and perhaps take away a chance for healing. If you are not ready for a change or for this kind of healing, if your resistance is still too great to at least allow it, please do not go to any energetic healer. You will go home dissatisfied.

This is often seen, for example, in work in the psychokinesiological field, where kinesiological testing is used to communicate with the subconscious and work on, among other things, traumas, negative beliefs, and so on. In the case of "self-sabotage" come changing or unclear answers up to the test inability. A good psychokinesiologist will have you say, for example, "I want to get well" and then test you. This way he can see if your subconscious sees it the same way or not. And our subconscious is the determining part, not our conscious.

**This could be your path as a patient. But what about your own application**?

Maybe you have always been interested in trying it yourself? To have a remedy at hand for you and your family, which you can use yourself at home?

Perhaps you have even, unknowingly, acted in this way? Ultimately, it is not so much a question of definition, but rather of perspective. A mother who puts her hand on her child's stomach or head when the stomach grumbles or the head hurts, conveys energy, information, harmonious vibrations. It does the child good, it will feel comfortable in the arms of the mummy and recover faster.

How do we want to describe this effect? As a miracle? So placebo? Is it the effect of warmth, compassion or resonance? In any case, it does not seem to take place on the material level. Thoughts, emotions, a smile, a kind word, a soothing gesture, a listening and a "laying on of hands" have effects that we can hardly describe on a purely material level. Everything vibrates, everything is information, everything is energy. Is the mummy an energetic healer?

What might your path look like?
Reiki, for example, is a typical entry into the world of energetic healing. Many private individuals, often after experiencing the gift themselves, seek out a Reiki master and teacher, have themselves introduced to the world of Reiki, work with them for a while, and then get initiated to be able to give Reiki themselves.

Or EFT. Many clients who came to a life coach or healer with anxieties, for example, have learned this method and it has continued to accompany them in their later lives without them always having to see a therapist.

But maybe you are also interested in reading up on the world of Bach Flower Remedies and finding the right flower essence for yourself or a family member?

I can only suggest that if you feel the desire to use your healing powers yourself, don't be afraid. Read up on the method you are drawn to. Join Facebook groups or study groups in your area. Attend a seminar on your topic sometime.

Under chapter 3 I have described a few types of energetic healing to you, perhaps you have already felt access to one or the other from your gut feeling.

# Self-discovery or "Who am I?"

**How do I find myself? This is a path that for some takes a lifetime and many never get there. Others are content and at peace with themselves, but have they found themselves? What is this "self"?**

I will describe you once my conception, as I understand the life.     We are souls, which make use of a body for a certain time, in order to collect experiences on this, our beautiful earth. One can go far into this topic, but I don't want to, it would go beyond the scope. However, if we are souls, then we cannot be the body we inhabit at the same time. Nor can we be the mind or spirit that we form only in the course of a life-time, some more, others less, through experiences, traditions through our ancestors, upbringing, education, social and moral values of the community in which we grow up and live. So if we only use our bodies and minds, who are we? Those who we really are are our souls. That is, the part of us that has begun the journey to earth and will leave it to return home.

I admit, this point of view is for many very getting used to up to moronic. Again, my request, do not judge too much, take it as a way to understand life.

---

**Body, mind and** soul¶

---

It is difficult to impossible for the mind to get out of thinking and values. The mind or "our spirit" is a tool. It evaluates everything on the basis of its thought patterns, its experiences made so far, which in turn is pre-programmed by the previously imparted beliefs of what is right and wrong. What is wrong in our society corresponds to the moral concepts in other societies. Animals, which are bred here in mass animal husbandry for the end consumer, are sacred in other countries. What is right, what is wrong? Who wants to decide this? It is always a valuation of our mind, shaped by the circumstances in which we live and have grown up.

Our soul, the part that we really are, does not judge. For it there is no good and evil, no right or wrong. It simply "Is". Another soul, which hurts me very much, is here to enable me as a soul the feeling of suffering and possibly forgiveness. Without this other soul this experience would not be possible for me. And in order to make experiences, I am born into exactly this body and family association.

At some point, both souls go home again. There, where everything consists only of love and there are no "good" and "bad" souls. If you have something to gain from this way of thinking, or at least would like to learn more about it, I recommend you take a look at Horst Tepperwein's publications.

# How do I find my healer?

There are many paths and they all have one thing in common: they are started with the first step. And you will not only go one way, you will go a second and a third at the end of the first way, you will leave some way already at the first fork. But what you will take with you, from every path, no matter how short, are the impressions. Just as even the shortest path through nature sends a flower, an insect, a ray of light or a bird's chirp to us, every meter will make you richer in experiences for the whole life.

# Possible
# Sources of information

Experiences of acquaintances and friends come first. This way you get impressions from people you know and hopefully can assess.

The formerly widespread forums on the Internet have become fewer in favor of Facebook and, more recently, Telegram.

If you have a Facebook account, you have access to many groups that have formed about certain diseases, therapy options, and so on. In well-run groups, you have smart people who are therapists themselves and will be happy to answer many of your questions. And you will find affected people there, people who suffer from the same symptoms as you and who have sometimes gone through years of visits to many doctors. So you will not only learn from fellow sufferers that they have the same problems, but also which path they have taken or are still taking to find a cure. However, I do not want to conceal the fact that there are also poorly managed groups in which many people "cavort" who have a lot of time and prefer to use it to quickly answer questions that are not asked without core competence. You will quickly understand what I mean.

On the Internet, you also have the option of landing hits with the right search terms. I prefer www.google.de because it is simply the most used search engine and intuitive to use. For example, enter the following search terms (depending on what you are looking for)

- Place of residence (if you want to limit the journey)
- Energetic healer
- Reiki, Akasha, ... (depending on your choice of the method you are looking for)
- Experience (if you have found a healer and want the assessment of others).

You should note with written down experiences on the Internet that someone is more inclined to write if he was not satisfied. The crowd of satisfied people does little work to communicate this to others. The dissatisfied are quicker to get their frustration off their chest. So a one-sided picture can quickly emerge. Nevertheless, it is a helpful source if certain "problems" are repeatedly raised with a healer.

Look at the Internet sites of the healers. You will get so a first or further impression of him. The choice of words, the self-portrayal, the description of his career and his methods. Does the site seem very commercial for profit or is the patient in the foreground? Do you feel on the same wavelength with what you see there?

And don't forget, even a healer, no matter how much he believes in love and light, has to eat, drink and pay rent. He usually has a very long own path of development behind him, from which you will benefit.

"Many healers have experienced firsthand over decades, which may lead you to him. You have before you, if you make the right choice, not someone who has his knowledge from a study, but whom life with all its "tasks" has
has shaped."
*(Maik Gollas, Information folder patients)*

# The thing with intuition

If you then have found a possible healer for you, you will feel in a first conversation whether there will be a cooperation or not. With an energetically working doctor or alternative practitioner you have an appointment, which is then paid by the health insurance or which you have to pay yourself as a self-payer. With a spiritual healer, spiritual working life coach, healer, medium etc. you are always self-payer.       ¶ Let the first hour, the first conversation work on you and if you can not build trust, your stomach or heart tells you no, then leave it thankfully with it. Everything has its time and the right healer will come into your life at the right moment.       ¶With this kind of work the chemistry must be right, the heart must be open for new impulses, for emotions and trust.

And once again my words, if the person you are looking for says something about you or your life, which you cannot "sign" at all, which causes indignation in you up to the inner or also shown aggressiveness towards him, then let it sink and look at the topic and the said with some distance once again, after the emotions have passed. And try for once not to "evaluate" the words, but only to take note of them. The healer or life coach perceives you "without a filter". He does not have the problem of having to look at you through your experiences and the filter of your (self-) perception. And always, when it hurts especially, the finger was exactly in the wound.

# Short legal excursion

**First of all, I am not allowed to give you legal advice or anything resembling legal advice. I will limit myself to naming and quoting some important laws that you should deal with in case of practicing.**

For home use, it does not matter to you if you lay hands on yourself or your family members and support their self-healing powers at their request. However, I would like to urge you to be careful about making "healing promises" or talking about "treatment" or "patients". Even more so when you write about your abilities in social media.

For "practicing" healers it looks even more "tightened". Here I would strongly recommend you to deal intensively with **§ 1 Heilpraktikergesetz** (HPG) and the **Heilmittelwerbegesetz** (HWG).

---

**A healer does not need permission according to the Heilpraktikergesetz in order to work.**

---

You can find more about this under
*https://www.dgh-ev.de/presse/geistiges-heilen-als-beruf-erst-seit-zehn-jahren-deutschland-legal.html,* a site of the "Dachverband Geistiges Heilen e. V." (DVGH).

The important and useful **fundamental decision of the Federal Constitutional Court** (BVG) was issued in 2004. The BVG had to decide on a constitutional complaint of a plaintiff against a decision of the Administrative Court (VG) Schleswig-Holstein and a decision of the VG Schleswig-Holstein as well as a previously issued decision of the district Schleswig-Flensburg. Under the file number **AZ 1BVR 784/03,** the

BVG stated in its decision that the healer does not practice medicine in the sense of the HPG and therefore does not need a permit for his activity according to this.

The conditions for this are described in detail. You can find the full wording on the SNB page to read and print out.
*(www.bundesverfas-*
*sungsgericht.de/SharedDocs/Entschei-*
*dugen/DE/2004/03/rk20040302_1bvr078403.html)*

A DVGH press release on this decision can be found on the association's website.
*(https://www.bundesverfas-*
*sungsgericht.de/SharedDocs/Entschei-*
*dungen/DE/2004/03/rk20040302_1bvr078403.html)*
Energetic healers outside the two professions (doctor, non-medical practitioner) regularly refer to this judgment in their work and practice, the Dachverband Deutscher Heiler e. V. (umbrella organization of German healers) and others point out that this should also be brought to the client's attention in writing, before the start of the "session", and that under no circumstances should a healing promise be made.
This then reads like this, for example:

<u>An important note for my work as a healer</u>

According to the verdict of the BVerfG, 1 BvR 784/03, dated 2.3.2004, I do not make any medical diagnoses, do not make any promises of healing and do not perform any therapy or treatment in the medical sense. My actions serve the recovery or the strengthening and support of the body's own self-healing powers and do not replace medical treatment.

*(Source_Flyer, www.zwei-strich-sinus.de)*

# Accompanying text and thanks

I would now like to release you from my world of thoughts and hope to have brought you some ideas, information and suggestions around energetic healing and its users. Do not worry if some of the approaches seem too "spiritual" or even "esoteric" to you. I would be happy if you would allow me and others to use them without judging the person. And who knows, maybe, one day in a distant time, you will feel like me.

Then you consume a book that you used to vehemently reject in one night and buy the next volume the next day. For me it was "Conversations with God" by Nils Donald Welsch.

It remains for me to thank you for your time and patience with me and my writing style.

I wish you a successful time and a good trip.